CH00555455

Your Keys to Total Breakthrough

DELE OLAWANLE

Baruch Press

DISCOVER YOUR PURPOSE
Copyright © 2006 by Dele Olawanle

Published by
Baruch Press
PO Box 1629
Croydon
CR9 9WW
info@baruchpress.co.uk

ISBN 1-900529-52-1

Cover design by *Topenoch*
Printed in the United Kingdom

CONTENTS

ACKNOWLEDGEMENTS

I give all glory to God for His grace upon my life and for inspiring me to write this book. The knowledge comes from Him because no one teaches like Him. Without Jesus, knowledge becomes sterile.

To all members of *Winners Kingdom*; a big thank you.

I am proud to dedicate this book to my beautiful wife, Bimbola, and our three wonderful children: Samuel, Joshua and Praise. It is hard enough being a practicing lawyer - not to talk of pastoring a church, lecturing and pushing forward in the field of gospel music. Without their patience, support and endurance, it would have been impossible to do this work.

I would like to thank God for my father in the Lord, Apostle Timothy Obadare who has shown so much love to me over the years and in whose ministry I cut my gospel teeth before I left to found *Winners Kingdom*.

Also, a special thank you to Pastor Sunday Adelaja of *God Embassy*, Ukraine, my friend, who read the draft and challenged me to raise this book to a new level.

Without their support, help, sense of humour, prayers, encouragement and endurance, this book would be sitting in my already overloaded library.

FOREWORD

Pastor Dele is a new generation of pastors that God is raising up in these end times. He is zealous, hungry and open to God to be a channel through whom God can carry out His will. Reading his book makes you know that this is a man of God and he is not just copying what other people are saying.

I highly recommend *Discover Your Purpose* to people who are hungry for God and the fulfilment of His purpose in their lives. May your purposes be fulfilled as you discover more of His will and purpose from this book.

Sunday Adelaja

Senior Pastor

The Embassy of the Blessed Kingdom of God for All Nations, Kyiv, Ukraine

"YOU ARE THE PURPOSE OF GOD
AND THE PURPOSE OF GOD
CANNOT BE HINDERED"

AUTHOR'S PREFACE

THE DREAM

It was around 5.00am on the 3rd of January, 2004. I had just finished my night prayers and was ready to go to bed.

As soon as I lay down, I began to have a dream. In the dream, I was invited to a church by a Pastor friend of mine to minister. As I got there, the church was full of people from all tribes and languages. They welcomed me joyfully as I had ministered there on several occasions as a gospel musician. They were ready to dance as usual but I told them that I was there in a different capacity: to preach the Word of God.

I mentioned the scripture reading for the message and the lady who accompanied me from the church I pastor in Hackney was about to read it when someone from the host church interrupted her. The latter read the wrong passage and would not allow my reader to read. At this juncture, I expected the host pastor to restore order but he seemed powerless.

I tried to continue with the message but there was so much disorder in the church that the pastor granted them a break of twenty minutes. At this stage I went to the Choir Department and realised it was full of people who were not really in the Lord. There were many of them and the Pastor came in and started eliminating them one by one. Many of them were doing nothing and were just hanging around. At the end, there were four instrumentalists left.

We went back to the church to continue with the service. As I mounted the pulpit again to preach, I noticed that there were just about eight people in the church. When I asked an usher where the others were, she told me they were upstairs partying. I left the church and stood outside. I lifted my eyes and saw all the church members dancing upstairs. The pastor was nowhere to be found.

Some people saw me where I was standing and said I should pray for them and I did. I asked them why the church members behaved that way and I was told that they were more interested in singing and dancing than hearing sound doctrine. They also told me that they had already arranged to have the party and they were in no mood to listen to the word of God.

At this point, I woke up. It was exactly 6.00am. I knew the meaning of the dream instantly.

THE MEANING OF THE DREAM

Sometimes in church, I tell my members in advance what the next message would be. The week before, I had told them that the message would be titled "The Total-Breakthrough Triangle". That was the same message I was prevented from preaching in the dream. I had this dream a day before I was due to preach the message in our church.

The meaning of the dream is simple. God is good and his mercies endure forever. He will always do whatever He says. Numbers 23:19 says, *"God is not a man that He should lie nor the son of man that he should repent..."* God has promised us good things through his word. The question then is, why are people suffering? Why is it that so many are not fulfilling their destiny? Why is it that some Christians are missing their purpose?

One major reason is that Christians today are more interested in the social aspects of the church than the spiritual. That is why many destinies remain unfulfilled. They are more interested in the Singles Night, Praise Night or Success and Blessing Seminars presented by unbelieving businessmen. Many people do not recognize their purpose in life. Many people do not have time for the things that would make them discover and fulfil their purpose in God.

As a musician who has sung in over 400 churches in the UK and abroad, I am a witness to this. My eyewitness account is that a lot of churches are now programming their services to suit the uninitiated, naïve, immature, unwise, careless and carefree 'born-again Christians' who are not aware that they are the purpose of God. The understanding I had through the dream was that the message is not only meant for the church that I Pastor but Christendom as a whole. That is why this message is presented as a book rather than a 40-minute sermon that would make minimum impact on lives and destinies.

Discover Your Purpose is about letting readers know that they are the purpose of God and that the purpose of God cannot be hindered. After discovering your purpose using the principles in this book, you would be able to overcome all problems, nightmares, bad luck, genetic or environmental diseases, generational curses, barrenness, misfortune, bad luck and the likes that has been plaguing your live over the years. You would then be able to fulfil your purpose in God.

I believe that by going through this book, you are in for an exciting time in the presence of God.

I welcome you into total breakthrough as you apply the principles in this book to your life.

It is well!

CHAPTER ONE

WHY PEOPLE SUFFER

"My people perish for lack of knowledge"

(Hosea 4:6).

Knowledge here does not only mean educational knowledge. It means knowing the principles to apply to your life; knowing what to do at a particular point in time. The Collins Paperback English Dictionary describes *knowledge* as *"the facts or experiences known by a person or a group of people."* It also describes knowledge as *"specific information about a subject."*

I announce to you that your life is a subject. The battles you are facing are subjects. You need to know specific information on how to win the battles; this time, in the spiritual realm.

I have seen it time and again that many Christians are suffering. God showed me through personal experience that it is impossible to have total breakthrough without first discovering your purpose in life and then applying some fundamental principles to one's life.

Christians today move from one church to the other looking for breakthroughs. Some have joined the occult in order to experience breakthroughs. Some have even decided not to attend church anymore because they are finding success difficult.

I submit here that the problem is not with God or the Church; the problem is with the individual. Breakthrough comes through a personal relationship with God, knowing God and depending on him through the storms of life. Breakthrough comes through recognising that you are the purpose of God, discovering your purpose and taking steps to fulfilling that purpose.

What I am about to unveil in this book is both theoretical and practical. That is why this book is titled, *Discover Your Purpose*. Only a consistent, meticulous and unbroken application of the principles that would be unveiled in this book will lead to total breakthrough that would make it possible for you to fulfil your purpose after discovering it.

Don't stop reading; fasten your belt as we embark on this spiritual voyage. You are just a few pages away from total breakthrough.

CHAPTER TWO

YOU ARE
THE PURPOSE OF GOD

Job said in Job 42:2 that *"I know that You can do everything And that no purpose of Yours can be withheld from you."* In saying this, Job was acknowledging the power and awesomeness of God. Job recognised, through personal experience, that the solution to his problems lied with God. He recognised that he was created for a purpose and that despite his adversity, God was able to turn his sorrow into joy.

God declared His power and greatness when He said the following through Isaiah:

> "But now, thus says the Lord, who created you O Jacob, And He who formed you, O Israel: "Fear not, for I have redeemed you: I have called you by your name. You are Mine. When you pass

through the waters, I will be with you; And through the rivers, they shall not overflow you. When you walk through the fire, you shall not be burned, Nor Shall the flame scorch you. For I am the Lord your God, The Holy One of Israel, your Savior; I gave Egypt for your ransom, Ethiopia and Seba in your place. Since you were precious in My Sight, You have been honored, And I have loved you; Therefore I will give men for you, And people for your life. Fear not, for I am with you; I will bring your descendants from the east, And gather you from the west; I will say to the north, 'Give them up!' And to the South, 'Do not keep them back!' Bring my sons from afar, And My daughters from the ends of the earth – Everyone who is called by My name, Whom I have created for My Glory; I have formed him, yes, I have made him". Bring out the blind people who have eyes, And deaf who have ears. Let all the nations be gathered together, And let the people be assembled. Who among them can declare this, And show us former things. Let them bring out their witnesses, that they may be justified; "You are My witnesses, " says the Lord, "Ands My servant whom I have chosen, That you may know and believe Me, And understand that I am He. Before Me there was no God formed, Nor shall

there be after Me. I, even I, am the Lord,
And besides Me there is no savior. I have
declared and saved, I have proclaimed,
And there was no foreign God among
you; Therefore you are My witnesses,"
Says the Lord, "that I am God. Indeed
before the day was, I am He; And there is
no one who can deliver out of My Hand; I
work, and who will reverse it?"

(Isaiah 43:1–13).

In the above passage, God declared that He
is the All in All. He declared that He is able to
protect us even when all human hope seems
lost. He promised us blessings and divine
intervention. He also told us through this
passage that when He works no man could
reverse it. What an awesome God!

The Bible is also littered with passages of
possibilities with God. In Luke 1:37, the Bible
says, *"For with God nothing shall be impossible"*
and in Jeremiah 32:27, God Himself said,
*"Behold, I am the Lord, the God of all flesh. Is there
anything too hard for me?"* What all these
passages point to is that there are endless
possibilities with God. Men and women
should therefore rely on Him absolutely.

People who realise that they are the purpose
of God behave differently. They have a

different approach to life. They are not worldly and they do not waste precious time because they know that the time is very short. They know and recognise that our God is a God of substitutes and can replace any man that fails to do His bidding.

Men of purpose do not joke aimlessly. They are serious-minded people with a different mentality. Recognise it from today that you are the purpose of God.

Let us now look at some people in the Bible who were conscious that they were the purpose of God:

DAVID

The bible says the following about David:

> "Then David spoke to the men who stood by him, saying, "what shall be done for the man who kills this Philistine and takes away the reproach from Israel? For who is this uncircumcised Philistine, that he should defy the armies of the living God?" And the people answered him in this manner, saying, "So shall it be done for the man who kills him." Now Eliab his oldest brother heard when he spoke to the men; and Eliab's anger was aroused against David, and he said, "Why did you

come down here? And with whom did you left those few sheep in the wilderness? I know your pride and the insolence of your heart, for you have come down to see the battle." And David said, "What have I done now? Is there not a cause?"

(I Samuel 17:26–30).

David knew that he was the purpose of God. Any man who is the purpose of God is alert to opportunity the moment they see it. If there is no opportunity, they create one. David understood that he had an unusual grace upon his life. Though not a trained soldier, he had killed a lion and a bear while tending the sheep. He recognised that it was God that gave him the strength to kill them, since lions and bears are naturally stronger than humans.

When David saw Goliath, he asked the people around him what would be the price for killing Goliath. They told him and Eliab, his brother, rebuked him for asking. He accused David of being proud. I want to say at this juncture that the borderline between pride and confidence is very thin. People often accuse confident people of being proud.

David was not dissuaded by the words of Eliab; he turned away from him to ask another person. Some of you will have to turn away from some people who are using their influence as your elders and friends to hinder God's plan for your life. David sensed that it was not pride moving him against Goliath but that he was the purpose of God in the situation. He saw a half chance and turned it to a full-blown opportunity. He killed Goliath and from that day his life was never the same again. The day you recognise that you are the purpose of God, your life will never be the same again; you will serve God with a greater passion. The day you realise that you are the purpose of God, you will stop wasting your time on things that do not profit.

ABRAHAM

> "Now the Lord had said to Abraham: "Get out of your country, from your family And from your father's house to a land that I will show you. I will make you a great nation; I will bless you And make your name great; And you shall be a blessing. I will bless those who bless you, And I will curse him who curses you; And in you all the families of the earth shall be blessed." "So Abraham departed as the Lord had spoken to him…"

(Genesis 12:1–4).

From this passage, one thing is very clear. Abraham had to leave a familiar territory to an unfamiliar zone. As a man who has sojourned abroad for some years, I know that it is not an easy thing to leave your father's house, your family and your country for another country. But it takes identifying that you are the purpose of God to do what Abraham did. He departed immediately, not after five years. He accepted that he was the purpose of God. For you to fulfil your purpose, you will need to deal with procrastination. The "tomorrow" you were talking about yesterday is now today.

The same thing happened to him in Genesis 22 when God asked him to sacrifice Isaac and he almost killed him. He was ready to do the will of God. How many times has God approached you to do something for Him and you had failed? If Abraham had disobeyed God, he would have missed his purpose. After embracing the purpose of God, you must be fully obedient to God's specific instruction. Partial obedience is still disobedience.

DANIEL

Daniel realised that he was the purpose of God when in Daniel 1:8, he purposed that he would not defile himself with the portion of the king's delicacies. He remained resolute in the face of adversity and in Daniel 6:9-22, He was thrown into the lion's den and yet he overcame. Remember what Job said above that the purpose of God could not be hindered.

SHADRACH, MESHACH AND ABEDNEGO

These three men realised that they were the purpose of God and in Daniel 3:4-15, they refused to bow down for the gold image that King Nebuchadnezzar had set up. Despite the threat of being thrown into the fiery furnace, they withstood the king and were victorious.

ATTITUDES OF PEOPLE WHO RECOGNISE THAT THEY ARE THE PURPOSE OF GOD

Having discussed the lives of some men in the bible who believed that they were the purpose of God, I would like to tell you that they have particular attitudes which gave made them victorious.

1. They are bold

We saw that David was a very bold person. Young but bold, untrained but bold, harassed but bold and despised but bold. For you to fulfil your commission as the purpose of God, you must be bold. Timothy 1:7 says, *"For God has not given us a spirit of fear, but of power and of love and of a sound mind."* If you are fearful, you will find it difficult to fulfil your purpose because Jesus did not shed his blood to raise cowards. Proverb 24:10 says *"If you faint in the day of adversity, your strength is small."* You must therefore be bold.

2. They are confident

We saw that the three Hebrew were confident even when they threatened to throw them into the fiery furnace. How confident are you?

3. They trust God unshakably

Daniel and Abraham demonstrated this by trusting God absolutely.

4. They are givers

People who recognized that they are the purpose of God are givers. Abraham and David demonstrated this by giving all they had to God. If you recognize that you are the purpose of God, you must trust Him with your possession.

5. They fear God

Joseph realized that he was the purpose of God and he did not sleep with Potiphar's wife despite having the opportunity to do so. David also repented after killing Uriah because he feared God.

6. They are resilient

People who know that they are the purpose of God do not give up easily. They fall and rise again. They believe what Psalm 34:19 says, *"Many are the afflictions of the righteous, But the Lord delivers him out of them all."*

7. They are faithful

People who recognize that they are the purpose of God are faithful.

8. They are obedient

Abraham is a good example of obedience. The moment God visited him and told him to leave his country, He did not procrastinate. He departed according to God's instruction and went to settle in the promised land.

9. They are humble

James 4:6 says, *"God resists the proud, But gives grace to the humble"*. People who realize that they are the purpose of God remain humble. They are not proud or arrogant. Jesus Christ is the quintessence of humility.

10. They have a very big vision

People who realise that they are the purpose of God have very big visions. They are never satisfied with the status quo. That was why Abraham left his country immediately. That was what made Joseph to flee from Bathsheba and that was what made David to kill Goliath not content with just looking after the sheep. Recognise today that you are the purpose of God and enlarge your vision. Your actions will follow your expectation.

CHAPTER THREE

HOW I DISCOVERED MY PURPOSE

I came to live in the United Kingdom in 1990 from my native Nigeria. Nothing prepared me for the shock that met me on arrival. I used to think that just landing in United Kingdom was enough to make me rich. It was on arrival that I found out that the more oceans you cross, the more nightmares you encounter.

I was a Project Manager in Nigeria and as a young man I was very comfortable. But somehow, I was not satisfied with the job I was doing in Nigeria. I saw no future in it. I tried to join the army thrice but was not successful. I then decided to travel abroad.

The jobs that were on offer on arrival were a shock to my system. From a Project Manager to a toilet and train station cleaner. I did this job for many years but found no fulfilment. I joined a Pentecostal Church and I started serving in the church. Coming from an Anglican background, I found the way of worship in the Pentecostal Church incredible. I could now pray, sing and rejoice without any inhibition. Thank you Jesus!

But after a while, I became stagnated in my thoughts. I used to say, "I have no ambition because God is my ambition." I was content to attend all the church services, work and go to bed. Indeed, God's people perish for lack of knowledge.

One day, the Holy Spirit ministered to me and said "Dele, do you know you would be more useful to me if you become educated?" That was when my eye of understanding opened. I started praying and seeking the face of God. I had a specific leading to study Law and become a lawyer. I went into the university. On the other hand, I knew without a doubt that I have been called to be a minister of the gospel. The usual feeling was to go to the Bible School rather than the University to study Law. But I shunned that thought.

I went to the University, completed the Law degree, went to the law school, did my training contract and today I am a Solicitor of the

Supreme Court of England and Wales! Imagine; if I had not discovered my purpose, I would have ended up as a train station cleaner.

Being a practicing lawyer did not stop me from pastoring *Winners Kingdom*, a church set up in August 2004. I discovered that a Scripture in Isaiah was for me:

> "The Spirit of the Lord God is upon Me, Because the Lord has anointed Me To preach good tidings to the poor; He has sent Me to heal the brokenhearted, To proclaim liberty to the captives, And the opening of the prison to those who are bound;"

> **(Isaiah 61:1).**

Today, this verse is being fulfilled in my ministry. When a church member or any member of the public comes to me asking for prayer, if it is a legal problem, I do not need to pray. I just tell them what to do. This is because it is not everything that needs prayer. Sometimes, what you need is knowledge. On the other hand, if it is a spiritual matter, I pray for them. Today, because of my dual calling of being a lawyer and pastor, I meet people that I never thought I would be able to meet. God is now raising me to a position of prominence both in the legal field and in the ministry.

When I attend prisons, police stations or detention centres in the United Kingdom, whether as a pastor or to see my clients, I know that the Lord has anointed me to proclaim liberty to the captives and to open the prison to those that are bound. Is it not strange that a former cleaner is now operating at this high level? It is a result of discovering my purpose and I can boldly say today that I am the purpose of God and I cannot be hindered.

Sometimes, people do ask me how I combine both roles and my simple response is: It is the grace of God. When you discover your purpose, the grace will be there.

CHAPTER FOUR

DISCOVER YOUR PURPOSE

Having realized that you are the purpose of God, you need to discover your *own* purpose. I have shown you how I discovered mine. Some people spend their whole life chasing the purpose of other people and by the time they realise their purpose, it is too late to fulfil it. You must know for sure what God wants you to do and what you are in the world to do. If not, you could spend the rest of your life chasing shadows rather than the substance.

Another reason why you have to discover your purpose is that history does not remember people because they are rich. It is not wrong to be rich or acquire millions in the bank. However, I discovered through reading the bible that people that were remembered in the bible were people who raised men rather than those who made much money. Many

Christians are now being diverted from their purpose in God through daily messages of prosperity as if that is the whole purpose of the gospel. As a result of that, they concentrate on the acquisition of wealth to the detriment of their purpose in God. Despite all the efforts being made, some fail to be rich and their relationship with God becomes weak.

I have preached it time and again that if all a man achieves is an educational qualification, much money, a family and many houses, that man has come to the world in vain. If you look at the houses on your streets, unless you know the owner personally, you would not know who owns it by just looking at them. That means, history does not remember people for their property because as soon as they die, it becomes another person's property.

Let us go into the bible and see men that were remembered:

ABRAHAM

Abraham was remembered not only for his riches but also for his demonstration of unshakeable faith in God. He is remembered today as the friend of God because he never doubted God.

JOSEPH

Joseph was not remembered for his wealth but as a man who succeeded despite all the odds and went ahead of his people to save a multitude of souls.

MOSES

Moses was not remembered for his wealth but he was remembered for delivering the children of Israel from Egypt, the land of bondage.

JOSHUA

Joshua was remembered for taking the children of Israel into the Promised Land.

DAVID

David was remembered as a friend of God and a great warrior.

SOLOMON

Though Solomon was rich, he was remembered for his wisdom.

THE APOSTLES

In Acts 17:6; the Apostles of Christ were described as *"These who turned the world upside down...."*. How did they turn the world upside down? They upset the status quo by preaching the word of God, attacking wickedness, unrighteousness, hypocrisy and immorality. They demonstrated the power of God by destroying the power of the enemy and setting the captives free. If all they had was riches, history would not have remembered them.

Peter and the rest of the Apostles also did great exploits in the mane of Jesus and for this they were remembered.

JESUS CHRIST

Jesus Christ did not have a child or home but He is the most important person in history.

POPE JOHN PAUL (II)

Outside the bible in our present age, Pope John Paul (II) did not have a child but he did his best for God. He opposed abortion and homosexuality throughout his time. It is common knowledge that governments of nations were afraid whenever he spoke.

As I mentioned above, it is not wrong to be rich but it is a foolish thing to think that earthly gain alone is an achievement. That is wrong, absurd and pure ignorance. Christians have to be wary of the deceitfulness of riches.

Real greatness comes through people that you are able to rise and change their lives for the better. As you read above, all the people mentioned were called for a particular purpose but they had to discover their purpose. Discovering your purpose will set you on the highway to fulfilling the discovered purpose. The people mentioned above would have missed their purpose if they had gone on a frolic of their own. What are you called to do?

CHAPTER FIVE

FULFILLING YOUR PURPOSE IN GOD

It is not enough to discover your purpose; you must make every effort to fulfil your purpose.

Daily, we see potentially great destinies being buried. Some of them die without fulfilling their purpose. Go to the graveyard and you would find that there are more talents there than among the living. Why? It happens when people do not know the way or the principles to apply towards fulfilling their purpose in God.

Today, people come into the world and waste years smoking, drinking alcohol, stealing, in prison, partying, doing the wrong courses in school, doing jobs that they do not like, marrying the wrong man or woman or being trapped in a wrong relationship or country. Before they know it, death comes and they are buried. Their memory is gone forever. They died without fulfilling their dreams. This is because dreams have a way of burying unwary dreamers.

Recalling the dream that led to my writing this book, we see that many in the church are unsure of their purpose. They are only interested in music and things that do not profit. So, it is possible for one to be a Christian, attend church regularly and still miss out on purpose.

Though I am a young man, I have been in church all my life. I have seen people moving from one church to the other not knowing their purpose. They move from revivals to conventions not knowing why they are there. Something in them tells them that they are the purpose of God but they do not know what to do in order to fulfil that purpose. Ecclesiastes 10:10 says *"If the ax is dull, And one does not sharpen the edge, Then he must use more strength; But wisdom brings success."* It is therefore not enough for you to realise that you are the purpose of God, you must know how to fulfil that purpose. It is therefore possible to do many things without doing the right thing.

In the following chapter, I will be discussing in much details three principles, which are called "The Total-Breakthrough Triangle" that would help you to fulfil your purpose and remove every obstacle on your path. Remember, you are the purpose of God and His purpose cannot be hindered.

CHAPTER SIX

PRINCIPLE 1:
THE WORD OF GOD

A common expression used for revelation is "The Word of God." In Biblical tradition, the term was first applied to prophecy and later came to describe the Law as communication from God. In the New Testament, it is used for scripture, for the Gospel and the Person of Jesus Christ.

In Christian tradition, the expression occurs in a loose, popular sense that implies *the inspiration of the Bible*. In John 1:1, *Logos* means a "divine word: a self-communicating divine presence that existed with God and was uniquely manifested in Christ." In Greek, *Logos* means both spoken word and pervading principle.

However, since I do not intend to go into theology in this book, the language will be simple. The Word of God as will be discussed here means all the things listed in the above paragraph. To a layman, the Word of God is the Bible and all that's contained in it from Genesis to Revelation. Every other thing is a top up.

The Word of God is the Word of life. Paul the Apostle wrote in Philippians 2:16 that *"as you hold on to the word of life…"*

Some Christians do not have a bible. Some families do not have a family bible. Some Christians attend the church without their bible. The bible is your power, strength and strong weapon. You must have one at home, while you get a pocket bible to carry about (instead of "Harry Potter"). Apart from failing to recognise that they are the purpose of God, many Christians do not know what knowing the Word of God and learning it by heart could do in their lives. It is not enough to pray; you must pray with the Word.

It is one thing to possess a Bible and another thing to read it. Read through the bible at first to know the stories. Then proceed to study the Bible. The Spirit of God will inspire you and help you to understand what you read (Job 32:8). You should also be interested in bible studies and cell groups. Buy tapes of messages from men and women of God and listen to it. Ask questions when you are not sure. Attend seminars and pray for understanding. Before you know it, you have become a 'Word-smith.'

> "Let the word of Christ dwell in you richly as you teach and admonish one another with all wisdom, and as you sing psalms, hymns and spiritual songs with gratitude in your hearts to God."

(Colossians 3:16).

The Word of God must dwell in you richly.

Have you noticed that some Christians do not attend Bible study meetings? On Sunday, you see the church filled to capacity with a bunch of praise worshippers dancing like butterflies. But they do not have time to learn. They do not have time to be taught. They then become a Martha in the kingdom, busy with things that do not profit and not having the power to overcome.

WHY YOU NEED TO KNOW
THE WORD OF GOD

1. The Word of God speaks different languages all the time

Many people believe that there is God just by looking at the massive expanse called earth with all its manifest wonders. But a deeper understanding of the Being called God will come when you study the Bible.

When asked why they decide one case this way and years later decide a similar case the other way, the Law Lords in England said, "The Law continually speaks to us." What they are saying is that, yes, we decided it that way years ago but today, we have a different understanding.

The same thing applies to the Bible. No one knows it all. The Bible continually speaks to us. That is why it is called "The Living Word." Hebrew 4:12 says, *"The word of God is living and active. Sharper than any two-edged sword, it penetrates even to dividing soul and spirit, joints and marrow; it judges the thoughts and attitudes of the heart."* Therefore, the Living Word is God and you must read it at all times not relying on residual knowledge or the Bible option you did at Secondary School years ago.

A theologian once said at a gathering that he does not need to read the bible, as he already knew the stories. I wanted to speak but knowing what I was going to say, the host Pastor beckoned to me to please sit down. That theologian was an academician who saw theology as a means to earn an income. However, as a child of God, you should be able to discern whether what you are being taught is spiritual or not.

2. To Have A Deeper Understanding Of God

"Study to show thyself approved unto God, a workman that needeth not to be ashamed; rightly dividing the word of Truth."

(2 Timothy 2:15 KJV).

Let us break this Scripture down:

'**Study**': This means to apply your mind to the learning and understanding of the words of the Bible especially by reading. It also means to investigate and carefully scrutinise. That was what the early disciples did. Studying brings a deeper understanding than mere reading. This is what you need to do also.

'Show thyself approved unto God': A lecturer who knows his subject will be valued. A student who knows the subject will be respected by his colleagues. A Christian who knows the Word will be known by God, because that means the Word of God is dwelling in Him.

I hasten to add that if God approves of you, your star will begin to shine and you will be well on the way to total-breakthrough. If you know the Word of God, no false prophet can quote a scripture from Genesis Chapter 51. You will know straightaway that Genesis has only 50 Chapters!

'A workman that need not to be ashamed, rightly dividing the word of truth': The bible records in Acts 4:13 that *"Now when they saw the boldness of Peter and John, and perceived that they were uneducated and untrained and ignorant men, they marveled; and they took knowledge of them, that they had been with Jesus."*

In our age, being with Jesus means knowing the Word of God. The Word brings boldness and confidence. Shame will disappear and you will do justice to the Word.

3. To Stop The Scourge Of Deceivers

"This know also, that in the last days, perilous times shall come."

(2 Timothy 3:1)

We are in the end times. There are many false teachers and false churches out there. If you are not rooted in the Word, you will be deceived and disappointed. Some of you reading this book have been deceived many times. Pulpit robbers with sugar-coated tongues have deprived you of money and possessions. Some of them have destroyed your relationships.

If you know the Word of God, you will know that the devil is a liar. You will be able to distinguish between his lies and God's truth. When they start using Maradona and Ronaldo as examples, your spirit will be quickened to the fact that we need Christian role models not socialites. Without knowledge of the Word, all you will be able to say when these false preachers are preaching is, "Preach it!"

Three years ago, I attended a revival meeting. On the first day, the preacher started talking about money and other worldly issues. There was in that congregation a lady who kept shouting, "Preach it Pastor!" She loved it.

The next day, a different pastor took the pulpit, preaching that holiness is the key to riches. I kept looking for the lady because I did not hear her "Preach it Pastor!" I concluded that she was absent. Much later, I was fortunate to spot her tucked into a corner, subdued by the message of holiness. When the altar call was given, she was the first to come out. The true Word of God brings total deliverance and emancipation from bondages.

> "But evil men and seducers shall wax worse and worse deceiving, and being deceived. But continue in the things which you have learned and are sure of, knowing through whom you learnt them"... All Scripture is God-breathed and is useful for teaching, rebuking, correcting and training in righteousness, so that the man of God may be thoroughly equipped for every good work."
>
> **(2 Timothy 3:13-17).**

You might have interpreted the "man of God" to be just pastors, but I believe that every man who has confessed Jesus Christ as his Lord and personal saviour is a man of God. Every woman who has confessed Jesus Christ as her Lord and personal saviour is a woman of God. If you are not a man or woman of the devil, then that Scripture includes you. You are a man of God and you need to study the Word of God to make you wise.

4. Total Deliverance

> "Wherein I suffer trouble, as an evil doer, even unto bonds, but the Word of God of God is not bound."

> **(2 Timothy 2:9).**

You may have been bound, but the Word of God (which cannot be bound) will set you free. When you do not have the Word in you, you are like a car without fuel. The amount of the Word of God in you will determine the extent of your victory. Knowing the Word and doing what it says will grant you deliverance.

In Matthew 4:1-10, Satan wanted to change the destiny of Jesus. The repeated use of the phrase *"it is written"* by Jesus put Satan to flight. Jesus did not only say *'it is written'*; he also mentioned what was written: *"Thou shall not tempt the Lord thy God"* (Verse 7). Jesus knew the Word before fasting and praying.

You cannot say 'it is written' if you have never read it. If you tell your situation or the devil that without knowing what was written,

Satan will ask you "where"? In short, he will become angrier with you.

Spend time in the Word of God and your victory will be assured.

5. Financial Prosperity.

Take for instance, the words of Paul the Apostle to the Philippians. In Philippians 4:19, he says *"My God shall supply your needs according to His riches in glory through Christ Jesus."*

Some Christians quote this scripture but they neglect the 'doing' aspect. The people to whom Paul directed this prayer were people who gave generously to support his ministry. I will quote from Paul's letter to the Philippians.

> "Moreover, as you Philippians know, in the early days of your acquaintance with the gospel, when I set out from Macedonia, not one church shared with me in the matter of giving and receiving, except you only; for even when I was in Thessalonica, you sent me aid (gifts) again and again when I was in need. Not that I am in need, but I am looking for what may be credited to your account." I have received full payment and even more; I am amply supplied, now that I have received

from Epaphroditus the gifts you sent. They are a fragrant offering, an acceptable sacrifice, pleasing to God."

(Philippians 4:17,18).

And then the verse we all love to quote:

"And my God will meet all your needs according to his glorious riches in Christ Jesus."

(Philippians 4:19).

When was the last time you blessed your pastor with a tie, a pair of shoes, suit, shirt, food or money? When was the last time you paid your tithe? Understanding the context in which that word was uttered will provoke you to giving. That would lead to God meeting all your needs. If you do not have the understanding, you will just be quoting the Word while squirming with envy when people with understanding are prospering.

We love to sing, "Abraham's blessings are mine," but do not pay tithes, offerings or remember to pay our vows. Some are more tight-fisted than the tortoise! (In African folklore, Mr. Tortoise was a miser who never gave). If you are not a giver, forget about Abraham's blessings.

6. *Judgement and Salvation*

The Word of God assures us of salvation. It also tells us about judgement. Knowing the Word of God will help you to examine your life regularly to see whether you are still in the faith. The Word of God is a microscope. It opens you up and then, sets you free. It would allow you to order your life as enumerated in Matthew chapters 24 and 25. It tells us that the end will surely come and that God will judge us.

WHAT YOU NEED TO DO NOW:

- Get a bible if you have none

- If the language used in your present Bible is not simple enough for you, get the New International Version or any version that is easy to understand.

- If there is a Bible written in your local language, get one.

- In addition, get the New King James Version or the King James Version for cross-referencing.

- Join a Bible-believing Church where sound doctrines are taught.

- Attend seminars and Bible studies.

- Join a Cell Group where the Word of God is discussed.

- Buy teaching tapes by men of God whom you know are not seeking their own.

- Ask for wisdom and understanding according to James1: 5.

- Then, become acquainted with the Word of God. You will notice significant changes in your life, which ultimately, will lead you to total-breakthrough and set you on the highway to fulfilling your purpose in God.

CHAPTER SEVEN

PRINCIPLE 2: PRAYER

This is the second chain in the total-breakthrough triangle. Jesus started with it and ended with it.

WHAT IS PRAYER?

After studying the Word of God, you need to apply it in prayer. Use the Word of God to talk to God. The Bible is a book of commandments, not suggestions. Prayer is the umbilical cord linking you (a child of God) to God Himself. Alas, some Christians do not pray or do not have time to pray. Some churches do not pray for up to ten minutes in their Sunday Service. It is all about music. Some Christians do not attend the Midweek Service. All they depend on is the 10-minute prayer offered last Sunday. Let me say at this juncture, that a prayer-less

Christian is susceptible to depression and confusion.

Prayer is the umbilical cord that connects us to God Almighty. Not just prayer but prayer through our Lord Jesus Christ. Prayer brings victory. Prayer does what God can do. This is to say, anything God can do, your prayer can do it. How wonderful it would it be if men and women would pray! Prayer is the vehicle on which our requests travel to God. Without prayer, your needs are just desires with no hopes of fulfilment. If you decide to start praying today, you are on the way to total-breakthrough. The God of heaven will help you.

The Hebrews in Egypt demonstrated the power of prayer in the Bible. God heard their groaning and delivered them from the hand of taskmasters. Elijah also demonstrated it. He prayed that it should not rain for three and a half years and it did not rain. Later, he prayed that it should rain and it rained. In Jesus' name, I command the rain of blessing and anointing upon your life.

WHY SHOULD I PRAY?

Without prayer, one's success will be limited. Without prayer, one is on a roller coaster to stagnancy. Without prayer, one is a householder in the kingdom called failure. The worst thing a Christian can do to himself is not to pray.

Philippians 4:6 says, *"Be careful for nothing; but in every thing by prayer and supplication with thanksgiving, let your requests be made known unto God."* From this passage, you will see that prayer is making requisitions for your needs to be supplied.

Jesus also gave us an important lead.

> "Ask and it shall be given you; seek and ye shall find; knock, and it shall be opened unto you; for every one that asketh receiveth; and he that seeketh findeth; and to him that knocketh it shall be opened."

> **(Matthew 7:7-8).**

This passage is self-explanatory. Jesus compared prayer to asking. If you ask, you receive. He also compared it to knocking. If you knock, the door shall be opened unto you. Prayer is also likened to seeking for something lost. If you seek it, you will find it.

HOW DO I PRAY?

Prayer does not always come naturally or easily. You need to learn how to pray. A prayer-life is like a baby: it grows. No one starts praying and becomes an expert on the same day.

It is always appropriate to begin your prayers with adoration, worshipping God for who He is. The more efforts you make, the better you become.

If you are just learning to pray, you can start with the Lord's Prayer, which Jesus taught his disciples on the mountain.

> "After this manner therefore pray ye: Our Father which art in heaven, Hallowed be thy name. Thy Kingdom come. Thy will be done on earth, as it is in heaven. Give us this day our daily bread. And forgive us our debts, as we forgive our debtors. And lead us not into temptation, but deliver us from evil: For thine is the kingdom, and the power, and the glory, forever, Amen."

(Matthew 6:9–13).

In the words of Dom Chapman, the key point is, "Pray as you can, and do not try to pray as you can't." In other words, do not try to pray like Elijah the day you start praying.

In the same way that relating with other people requires time and energy, prayer also places a demand on our time and effort. It needs to become part of our daily lives: a habit, a routine, an addiction, a necessity and a must-do. Prayer is harder than work. It is therefore hard work. It requires discipline, persistence, resilience and undiluted focus.

Many times, when it comes to praying, we become tired, weak, and weary like the disciples in the Garden of Gethsemane. That is when you should get up and realise that the prowler, Satan, is at work. The more you pray, the more you experience God's power and presence, the more you become interested in prayer.

Prayer is like a child just born into the world. At the initial stage he is innocent, but grows to become an important personality. That is how prayer grows. An innocent, naïve, powerless, confused, disillusioned, cowardly brother of yesterday suddenly becomes an evangelist, winning souls all over the world. Prayer knows no limits when it starts growing.

Do you want to be great and successful? Prayer is the key! As you decide to pray, do the following:

1. Confess and forsake your sin:

You need God to forgive you your sins before your prayers can be answered. You must confess them. Proverb 28:13 says *"He that covereth his sins shall not prosper: but whoso <u>confesseth and forsaketh them</u> shall have mercy"*. It is not enough to confess your sin. You must stop sinning. There has to be a finality to sin. Don't confess your sin before God when you are praying – only to then go back to do the same. Your prayers would be hindered if you do not stop sinning.

2. Forgive others:

Whenever you are about to pray, you must forgive those who have offended you. The Bible says in Matthew 7:14 that *"if ye forgive men their sins, your heavenly father will also forgive you."* So, you must forgive others and your heavenly Father will then have mercy on you. Forgiveness must also be total. You have probably been wounded, but I pray that the Almighty God will heal the wounds that were created by the hurt.

3. *Posture in prayer:*

You can pray by kneeling, standing, lying or sitting down. Whatever posture makes you comfortable are the one you should adopt. It is always better to stand or kneel so that your discomfort would prevent you from falling asleep especially when praying at night. Do not be a Jonah in prayer. Jonah (who was on assignment for God) was sleeping on duty. Sleeping when you should be praying is an invitation to spiritual nightmares, which would manifest in the physical as failure. It is also good to close your eyes while praying to avoid distractions. Have you seen people who open their eyes during prayer? They find it difficult to concentrate. Closing your eyes in prayer affords total concentration. It invokes an undiluted passion in prayer. Have you never closed your eyes in prayer? Try it.

WHERE SHOULD I PRAY?

Everywhere. In I Timothy 2:8, Paul the Apostle wrote: "*I will therefore that men pray everywhere, lifting up holy hands, without wrath and doubting.*" Pray everywhere but do not start binding the devil when you should be working for your employer. Be sensible. Apply wisdom. Do not leave your desk and start binding the devil in a shared office. You are likely to be dismissed. There is a time for everything.

HOW OFTEN SHOULD I PRAY?

All the time, as God gives you the grace. Paul the Apostle wrote in 1 Thessalonians 5: 17 that we should *"pray without ceasing."* Know that our God never sleeps or slumber. Call on Him anytime, anywhere and He would answer you. But as mentioned above, apply wisdom.

It is always good to find a time that you can regularly spend in prayer; a time when you will not be interrupted. Unless you are expecting an emergency call, do not pick up the phone when you are praying. It is a satanic strategy, especially in the Western World. Keep your prayer short to start with. As time goes on, you will develop more energy to pray. Aim at 20-30 minutes and try to combine it with reading the Bible. Remember, the Word of God is the sharp sword that cuts through your problems and needs. Use it in prayer. As time goes on, you will be able to pray for a longer period (including praying throughout the night- called 'Night Vigil').

WHAT TO DO NOW

- Thank God for his manifold blessings.

- Sing praises. If you do not know any worship songs, get worship tapes from Christian stores.

- Ask for forgiveness of your sins.

- Present your requests to God in faith.

- Thank him for answered prayer.

- Pray every day and do not stop.

CHAPTER EIGHT

PRINCIPLE 3: FASTING

The third thing you need to do is to be able to fast. This is the third chain of the Total-Breakthrough Triangle (Not with orange juice, as some pastors are teaching). This is because Jesus said in Mark 9:29 that some problems cannot go away but through prayer and fasting. Your pastor or your prophets cannot do it for you. Fasting is a "Do-it-yourself" activity.

I remember when I was growing up in Africa. Some friends and I went to a man who said he was a prophet. He said he would fast seven days for each of the three of us, totalling 21 days. He was going to start the fasting the next day, which was a Monday. I felt that he had to be a Superman. Out of curiosity, I decided to check him out two days later. On getting to his house, the door was unlocked. I entered his living room and there he was, drunk and covered in his own vomit. That was the last time I ever saw him. (I never told my friends).

Some Christians are still in that state of ignorance, paying prophets salaries to fast for them. Stop a minute and think: how many people can your prophet or prophetess fast for? Love it or hate it, some problems cannot go away without it. Nobody can do it for you; you must do it yourself.

WHAT IS FASTING?

Fasting is choosing to avoid eating (as a religious observance). You avoid eating from 12.00 am to 6.00 pm in the evening. You may want to end your fast at 12.00 pm or 3.00 pm as a beginner. That means you must not wake up at night to have a drink on the day you are proposing to fast. It involves abstinence from all food to show dependence on God and submission to His will. It is a devout practice, which acts as a potent aid to prayer. Luke 2.37 says, *"And she was a widow of about fourscore and four years, which departed not from the temple, but served God with fasting and prayers night and day."*

Fasting has different purposes in the Bible and some of them are as follows:

1. Mourning for the dead

"And they took their bones, and buried them under a tree at Jabesh, and fasted seven days."

(1 Samuel 31.13).

2. Expressions of repentance from one's sins

"Now in the twenty and fourth day of this month the children of Israel were assembled with fasting, and with sackclothes and earth upon them."

(Nehemiah 9.1).

3. For Intercession

"David therefore besought God for the child and David fasted, and went in and lay all night upon the earth."

(2 Samuel 12:16).

4. For God's aid

"Then all the children of Israel, and all the people, went up, and came unto the house of God, and wept, and sat there before the Lord, and fasted that day until even, and offered burnt offerings and peace offerings before the Lord."

(Judges 20.26).

5. For Personal reasons

"My knees are weak through fasting; and my flesh faileth of fatness."

(Psalm 109:23).

6. As a periodic liturgical observance

Periodic public service officially commanded by God or prescribed by the church:

"Thus saith the Lord of hosts; The fast of the fourth month, and the fast of the fifth, and the fast of the seventh, and the fast of the tenth, shall be to the house of Judah joy and gladness, and cheerful feasts; therefore love the truth and peace."

(Zechariah 8.19).

7. *As a natural discipline for spiritual enablement*

> "And when he had fasted forty days and forty nights, he was afterward hungry."

> **(Matthew 4:2 KJV).**

> "And Moses went into the midst of the cloud, and gat him up into the mount: and Moses was in the mount forty days and forty nights."

> **(Exodus 24.18).**

8. *To thwart the enemy's agenda*

> "Go gather all the Jews that are present in Shushan and fast ye for me and neither eat not drink three days, night or day: I also and my handmaid will fast likewise: and so will I go in unto the King, which is not according to the law: and if I perish, I perish."

> **(Esther 4:16)**

WHY SHOULD I FAST? (IS PRAYER NOT ENOUGH?)

Prayer without fasting is not enough for some problems. Jesus said in Mark 9:29 that *"this kind can come forth by nothing, but by prayer and fasting.*" What Jesus meant was that some problems cannot go away or be solved unless you fast. I once saw a *New International Version* Bible where the word "fasting" was missing. (If that is the Bible you have, add fasting to it immediately! That passage is a very lazy interpretation.) Let me dwell further on why Jesus made the statement.

Jesus went to the Mountain of Transfiguration in Mark chapter 9. He was apart from the other disciples, praying and fasting. The disciples were probably eating and drinking. So, Jesus came down from the mountain and saw the scribes arguing with the disciples.

They had brought to the disciples a child that was possessed by a dumb and deaf spirit, but the disciples could not heal him. Without much ado, Jesus cast out the spirit that had been troubling the child from his youth. When the disciples wondered and asked Jesus why they could not cast it out, he then replied that only prayer and fasting could do it (v29).

Your problems will argue with you if you cannot fast. Your sickness may remain. Enemies and Satan himself will question you on your faith. Any Christian that cannot fast will keep arguing with the scribes just like the disciples: full of theory and stories but no power.

Are you ready to have Total-breakthrough? Get into fasting and you will become a terror to Satan. A bold facade cannot give you victory, but boldness laced with fasting and prayer will.

HOW SHOULD I FAST?

Fasting starts at midnight until 6.00pm the next day. That was what I learnt from observing my mother and many servants of God that I served under. No breakfast. No orange juice or tea in the morning. If you are not able to fast until 6.00, you may decide to end the fast at 12.00pm or 3.00pm.

Initially, you may find it difficult. Please see your doctor if you are an ulcer patient. You may initially experience headache, unusual urge to eat, tiredness and so on. Do not let this put you off. You will soon get used to it.

You may start by fasting till 12.00pm and then have your Cornflakes. You may then progress the next time you want to fast till 3.00pm until you are able to fast without eating until 6.00pm.

SOME RULES ON FASTING

Many Christians have been fasting for many years without results. This could be because they have not been observing rules on fasting. Many churches declare a period of fasting without telling the congregation what to do. They forgot that some are Muslim converts who used to have breakfast while fasting. Others used to be idol worshippers that have never been to church all their life. People must be taught what to do, why they should do it and how to do it. A complete fast is a complete and literal denial of self.

Isaiah 58 is the fasting chapter. Let us examine what it says and discover the many benefits of fasting when done God's way.

> "Cry aloud, spare not; Lift up your voice like a trumpet; Tell My people their transgression, and the house of Jacob their sins. Yet they seek me daily, and delight to know my ways, as a nation that did righteousness, and did not forsake the ordinance of their God. They ask of me the ordinances of justice; they take delight in approaching God. Why have we fasted, they say, and you have not seen? Why have we afflicted our souls, and you take no notice?"

(Isaiah 58:1-4 NKJV).

The above passage is saying that servants of God should speak out and not keep quiet in order to tell Christians why their prayers are not being answered. In the above passage, it says we should tell Christians their sins. They seek God daily and want to know the way of God as if they are righteous and have not forsaken the laws of God. They profess to want justice and total-breakthrough and love fasting. But having fasted many times with no change in their situation, they wonder why they fasted and God did not answer them. They want to know why God ignored them.

God then responded in verse 3, *"in the day of your fast you find pleasure, and exploit all your labourers"*. Let me explain.

"FINDING PLEASURE"

The time of fasting is a time of consecration. That is, you must set yourself apart, abhor filthiness and be holy. Some Christians do not set themselves apart.

Sex and fasting:

Pleasure could include having sex with your partner before, during and immediately after fasting. (Sexual relation is only permitted for husband and wives. People who are not married and are having sex are committing sin whether engaged, common-law wife or common-law husband. You therefore need to officially sanctify your relationship).

> "After Moses had gone down the mountain to the people, he consecrated them, and they washed their clothes. Then he said to the people, "Prepare yourselves for the third day. Abstain from sexual relations."

(Exodus 19:14-15).

The New King James Version says:

> "So Moses went down from the mountain to the people and sanctified the people, and they washed their clothes. And he said to the people, "Be ready for the third day; do not come near your wives."

(Exodus 19:14-15 NKJV)

Whatever Bible version you are reading, the instruction is very clear, no sex while fasting.

Having sex immediately before, during or after fasting may weaken the spiritual potency of prayer. Paul the Apostle gave us some blueprint on how to handle sex and fasting in his letter to the Corinthians.

"The wife does not have authority over her own body, but the husband does. And likewise the husband does not have authority over his own body, but the wife does."

(I Corinthians 7:4).

What this passage is saying is that your wife's body belongs to you and vice versa.

"Do not deprive one another except with consent for a time, that you may give yourselves to fasting and prayer; and come together again so that Satan does not tempt you because of your lack of self control."

(I Corinthians 7:5).

What this passage is saying is that a couple should be able to have sex whenever they want. However, they may deprive each other of sex in order to fast and pray for total-breakthrough. Nevertheless, he went further to say your fasting must not keep you away from your spouse to the extent that you give the devil a chance to lead you into sin. So you need your partner's consent in order to fast. Fasting must be by agreement. What God has joined together let fasting not put asunder!

Still, I have my reservations. What about a

spouse who does not want to fast? Should I wait until he or she agrees before I fast? The answer is no.

For people with unbelieving spouses, the issue of fasting should be handled with wisdom. If not carefully handled, it could destroy your relationship. Ensure that you help your husband or wife to understand why you have to fast at reasonable intervals.

Some claim to fast while they also drink alcohol, smoke cigarettes, kiss and engage in other unholy acts. The time of fasting requires holiness, concentration and undiluted focus.

Exploiting your workers

This is what I call "robbing and praying." Some believers claim that they are fasting and yet do not pay their workers what is rightly theirs. Many employers, supervisors and bosses are guilty of this. This issue is the factor that has been hindering your prayers.

Some businessmen and women cheat their customers. They are acting like Pharisees and it is dangerous. If this applies to you, change this evil habit. Some others cheat people out of their rights or embezzle money while fasting. It has been hindering your prayers.

Strife, debates and fighting

> "Indeed you fast for strife and debate, and to strike with the fist of wickedness. You will not fast as you do this day, to make your voice heard on high"
>
> **(Isaiah 58:4).**

There are also Christians who behave like tigers while fasting, abusing everybody at work. When asked why you are in an angry mood, you say 'I am fasting'. Some engage in gossips while fasting while others beat up their wives or slap their husbands. You have just blown it. The Bible says if this is what you call fasting, the heavens cannot hear you. You must change.

Wrong show

> "Is it a fast that I have chosen, a day for a man to afflict his soul? Is it to bow down his head like a bulrush, And to spread out sackcloth and ashes? Would you call this a fast, and an acceptable day to the Lord?"
>
> **(Isaiah 58:5).**

The time of fasting is a time to humble yourself before God, not before man. Some like to show off to others when they are fasting.

God is saying that an outward show of fasting is not acceptable unto Him.

The right things

> "Is this not the fast that I have chosen: To loose the bonds of wickedness, to undo the heavy burdens, to let the oppressed go free, and that you break every yoke?"

> **(Isaiah 58:6).**

The time of fasting is the time to be fair and to hate injustice. The time of fasting is the time to forgive those who offended you. The time of fasting is the time to leave wickedness and become a good Christian – not during fasting alone as a permanent outcome of your fast.

WHAT SHOULD ACCOMPANY YOUR FAST?

> "Is it not to share your bread with the hungry, and that you bring to your house the poor that are cast out; When you see the naked that you cover him, And not hide yourself from your own flesh?"

> **(Isaiah 58:7).**

The time of fasting is the time to give to the poor, the hungry and your relations. It is a good practice to even calculate the amount you would have spent on food during fasting and give it to the church. This is called "fast offering."

Marion G. Romney said: "One of the important things the Lord has told us is to be liberal in our payment of fast offerings. I would like you to know that there are great rewards for so doing – both spiritual and temporal rewards." Russell M. Nelson also said, "At least once a month, fast and pray and contribute generous fast offerings. We will be blessed and protected from apostasy by so doing."

THE RESULTS OF TRUE FASTING

"Then your light shall break forth like the morning, your healing shall spring forth speedily, and your righteousness shall go before you; the glory of the Lord shall be your rear guard."

(Isaiah 58:8).

Whenever you fast, as you should, you will have total-breakthrough. Your star will shine as mentioned in Isaiah: *"Arise, shine; for your light has come! And the glory of the Lord is risen upon you" (Isaiah 60:1).*

You will then be healed speedily as your righteousness in God through Jesus Christ will cause your requests to God to be granted.

> "Then you shall call, and the Lord will
> answer; you shall cry, and He will say,
> "Here I am". "If you take away the yoke
> from your midst, and the pointing of the
> finger, and speaking wickedness."

(Isaiah 58:9).

If you abandon wickedness and you fast as you should, your voice will attract God's attention. You will have a voice that the heavens listen to. I want a voice like that. The voice that says it should not rain (like Elijah did) and the heavens listened.

> "If you extend your soul to the hungry
> and satisfy the afflicted soul, then your
> light shall dawn in the darkness, and your
> darkness shall be as the noonday."

(Isaiah 58:10).

This verse is referring to giving to the less privileged during fasting. If you do, God will make a way for you.

> "The Lord will guide you continually, and
> satisfy your soul in drought, and
> strengthen your bones; you shall be like a
> watered garden, and like a spring of
> water, whose waters do not fail."

(Isaiah 58:11).

This passage promises God's guidance, meeting all your needs and empowerment. If you fast (as you should do), everything concerning your life will occur at the right time and the bands of stagnancy will be broken.

> "Those from among you shall build the old waste places; you shall raise up the foundations of many generations; and you shall be called the Repairer of the Breach, The Restorer of Streets to Dwell in."
>
> **(Isaiah 58:12).**

If you fast, as you should, you will become a Nehemiah who would rebuild your own gate of Jerusalem. Do you know this passage promises you unsurpassed greatness? You will become just like Joseph in his father's house. Are you ready for it? Go on and make it in Jesus' name.

CONCLUSION

Brethren, you must recognise that you are the purpose of God. Having recognised that you are the purpose of God, you must discover your *own* purpose. It is very important that you discover your own purpose so that you do not chase shadows all your life. Having discovered your purpose, you must then apply these three principles to enable you to have total-breakthrough.

If you are not ready to use this three-pronged approach to tackling your problems, you may find success difficult and it could hinder your purpose in God. You must know the Word of God, pray and fast regularly.

The modern 'softly, softly' approach to Christianity has robbed many Christians of power. Some pastors are even afraid of preaching about witches and wizards. Some ministers are afraid of casting out demons, when it should be *'Like master, like servants.'*

Jesus spent a good part of his ministry casting out demons. Are you able?

Prayer is vital. Prayer with the Word is thunderous. Prayer and fasting loaded with the Word is more than atomic bomb. These three principles would help you to fulfil your God given destiny.

I encourage you to cultivate the habit of using this three-pronged approach of lethal spiritual strategy to confront your problems.

I believe you have been blessed through reading this book. Apply these principles and walk into total-breakthrough in Jesus' name.

Remember, you are the purpose of God and his purpose cannot be hindered!

If you have been blessed by the reading of this book and you want some more copies, want to make some comments or you want to know more about the ministries of Winners Kingdom, please contact us through the following:

Telephone:
07956 54 34 38

E-Mail:
info@winnerskingdom.org.uk

By post:
PO BOX 720

DAGENHAM

RM10 7WF

UNITED KINGDOM